cd track listing:

disc 1

1. Guided Relaxation 7:15

2. Earth Meditation 32:07

3. Guided Relaxation 7:15

4. Air Meditation 24:00

disc 2

1. Guided Relaxation 7:15

2. Fire Meditation 22:54

3. Guided Relaxation 7:15

4. Water Meditation 37:25

stacey demarco

earth air fire water

a 40-day and 40-night
transformative healing journey

BLUE ANGEL®
PUBLISHING

earth air fire water

Published by Blue Angel Publishing®
80 Glen Tower Drive, Glen Waverley,
Victoria, Australia 3150
E-mail: info@blueangelonline.com
Website: www.blueangelonline.com

Edited by Jamie Morris

Blue Angel is a registered trademark of Blue Angel Gallery Pty. Ltd.

ISBN: 978-0-9872041-3-4

contents

The Elements..7
Elements Questionnaire...10
Checking your Score...15
Embarking on your 40-day & 40-night Elemental Healing Journey......17

EARTH...21
AIR...73
FIRE..125
WATER..177

Summary of Traditional Correspondences for the Elements...............229
Australian Alternatives to Elemental Directions and Associations......231

About the Author..233

the elements

the elements of earth, air, fire and water are the foundation for all matter. Therefore, we, whose bodies are made of matter, naturally contain these four elements within our physical selves. But as living beings that are part of the wider universe, we also embody these elements in a more energetic and spiritual sense. While each of us is a unique and beautiful mixture of all four elements, we tend to be characterised by one or two dominant elements, whose inherent qualities are expressed in our personality traits, attitudes and preferences in life.

When in the correct alchemic balance, the elements support us in being what we are born to be. But when they are out of balance, they may create obstacles that block our path. Since we are each unique, the balance of elements that is ideal for one of us will not be the same as the balance that is best for another. However, by considering the interplay of the elements in our own lives, we may be able to spot areas in which we are not achieving our best individual balance and we have an opportunity to change.

For example, if we find that we are having trouble taking action when we see that it's called for, it may be that we have an overdeveloped earth element or an underdeveloped fire element. By tapping into the energy of each element and working with it consciously, we can address such personal imbalances. We might discover ways to bolster our strongest element(s) and strengthen those that are less prominent in our personal make-up. In this way, finding our best elemental balance may help reach our full potential, while also bringing a general sense of equilibrium and happiness to our lives.

You may have heard of a fifth element, "ether." However, the qualities that are sometimes assigned to ether – that of a spiritual animating force – can be expressed in a four-element system, like the one I'm using here, by combining the actions of the elements of fire and air. Therefore, the four elements of earth, air, fire and water do completely cover all the aspects of our spiritual experience. It's useful to remember, also, that in this four-element system the more active elements of life – air and fire – are seen to act upon the more passive elements of water and earth. For example, the Stoic philosophers believed that the Creator (God, Logos) was made of a primordial fire that generated the four elements as we know them. (Think of the scientific concept of the Big Bang, and you'll get their drift).

The Greek Stoic philosopher Zeno considered all things to be "solid", and saw fire as the initial solid – followed by air, water and eventually earth. His branch of Stoicism believed that the soul itself is made of fire – an idea that we still see today in the connected notions that our soul is situated around or within our heart, which, in turn, is the seat of those "warm" fiery emotions, passion and love.

Another Greek thinker, Empedocies (490-430 BC), also promoted the idea that everything in the universe, including man, is composed of four elements. But he added the quite beautiful idea that these elements are either brought together or pulled apart by two forces that he called "Love", which he saw as attracting the elements, and "Chaos", which he saw as separating them. Imagine, everything in our universe being affected by these two energies – even at a physical level!

In the East, we find Buddhism mentioning four elements extensively, as well. And the Indian system of Ayurveda describes body types on the basis of hot/cold (fire), wet/dry (water) and earthy/airy (earth and air).

Yet, whilst the idea of the four elements is certainly nothing new as we have seen, we may have forgotten that they are important to us, now. As modern people with modern issues and problems, we might ask, "Why bother investigating how our 'energetic' selves are composed elementally?"

Let's turn back to the Ancient Greeks for another moment. From them we receive the idea that it is a wise move to be curious about ourselves. "Know thyself" is the most famous of the ancient Greek Delphic maxims and is considered to be the foundation of much of philosophic thought. This concept, which has stood the test of time, is as relevant now as it was thousands of years ago. Considering our elemental tendencies offers us an avenue to learn more about ourselves and thus grow and positively change if we need to.

Knowing more about how the elements of earth, air, fire and water blend in our personal energetic make-up can give us an insight into what makes us strong and unique – and help us determine our shadows or blind spots. This knowledge, which helps us identify our natural positives and negatives, can also help us reduce the things we do that create difficulties for us and increase those that create positive experiences. Additionally, we can further boost our own energy levels by plugging into places that resonate with the elemental energies we need. This can deliver a surge of this element's energy at its most powerful, which is not only convenient but usually pleasurable.

And, finally, we can connect to whatever we see as our Higher Power more deeply and peacefully if we discover the easiest gate to pass through – that of our primary element. The CDs that come with this book contain meditations specific to each of the elements that will assist you to do just that.

take this elements questionnaire to learn your dominant element(s)

Choose the answers that best describe you and your behaviours at present. While there may be several answers that are relevant to you, for each question, choose the one closest to your true preference. Be as honest as you can. Take your time considering the often-subtle differences between the options.

1. When I choose to go on a holiday, I would usually prefer
    a) a cruise or holiday by the beach.
    b) trekking or skiing in the mountains.
    c) an adventure in the bush or an animal safari.
    d) a fast paced holiday, possibly in the city.

2. My favourite natural landscape would be
    a) a desert with red rolling sand dunes or an erupting volcano.
    b) a beautiful river scene or an incredible underwater environment.
    c) a lush green rainforest or a peaceful, flower-dotted meadow.
    d) the high vistas of a mountain range or the approach of a storm.

3. I consider myself
    a) even tempered.
    b) quick tempered.
    c) slow to anger, furious when I do get angry, tending to hold a grudge.
    d) a good communicator, so I rarely get angry, and if I do, I forgive easily.

4. I am (choose only the most dominant)

a) passionate about what I believe.

b) grounded, rational and practical.

c) curious and very interested in learning.

d) flexible and open to new ideas.

5. If I have to make an important decision, I tend to

a) make it quickly and decisively.

b) take my time considering the options and maybe even overthink it.

c) just go with the flow.

d) research it first to make a good decision.

6. The weather I like best is

a) hot and dry.

b) stormy and windy.

c) all types of weather.

d) rainy days and humidity.

7. Food for me is

a) fuel.

b) one of the greatest joys in life.

c) a way for my body to be nourished and taken care of.

d) something to be savoured with a fine wine in a beautiful environment.

8. When things are not going well in my life, I feel

a) heavy and stuck.

b) ungrounded and confused.

c) bored, unfocused or drama-filled.

d) overwhelmed or like I'm going nowhere fast.

9. At my most balanced and happy, I feel

a) peaceful and in the flow.

b) efficient, focused and motivated.

c) creative and clear.

d) secure, productive and resilient.

10. One of my favourite everyday things to do is

a) go barefoot.

b) have a bath or shower.

c) read a book.

d) work on a new project or discover something new.

11. If I am worried, I tend to

a) lose weight because I lose interest in food.

b) gain weight because I do not care about the quality of what I eat.

c) lose sleep and get angry that I have got myself into this situation.

d) get very emotional and not think clearly.

12. If I could have my ideal home it would be situated

a) by the sea, lake or river

b) on an open piece of land or top of a hill, with plenty of fresh breezes.

c) in a thriving city, with lots to see and do.

d) among huge trees, with wildlife and a beautiful garden.

13. I admire people who can
a) separate their emotions from their intellect and act intelligently.
b) drive themselves and others and be passionate about what they do.
c) consistently balance their lives and achieve things without great force.
d) put their family first and provide well for them.

14. I prefer these colours:
a) white, pastels and silver.
b) blues and grey.
c) greens and natural shades.
d) bright yellows, orange and red.

15. I find it easier to open up all my senses
a) in a long, hot bath or by the sea.
b) by eating food or within the bush or forest.
c) when I am travelling or when I am in a place that is very open and free.
d) when I am totally and happily immersed in an activity or project.

16. I consider the following value to be most important:
a) freedom.
b) emotional expression.
c) motivation.
d) security.

17. I do not like feeling

    a) rushed and asked to make changes quickly.

    b) that I am being micromanaged.

    c) unfocused and without direction.

    d) stuck and misunderstood.

18. An ideal gift for me would be

    a) fragrance or books.

    b) a workshop in something I'm interested in getting better at.

    c) something to make my home or garden more beautiful.

    d) a chance to go whale watching or a lunch by the sea.

19. I feel repelled by people who

    a) are very dogmatic and inflexible.

    b) have no goals and just drift along.

    c) don't think about anything deeply.

    d) are pushy and get angry easily.

20. Going by my first impressions, I think I most embody the element of

    a) earth.

    b) air.

    c) fire.

    d) water.

checking your score

Look back over your Elements Questionnaire and write down how many answers you gave for each of the four colours. Award one point for each answer. Tally your results, and then consult the following elemental correlations.

If you got mostly answers with this colour, which represents EARTH, you are Earth element dominant.

If you got mostly answers with this colour, which represents AIR, you are Air element dominant.

If you got mostly answers with this colour, which represents FIRE, you are Fire element dominant.

If you got mostly answers with this colour, which represents WATER, you are Water element dominant.

If you scored very high for **one particular element** in comparison to the others, you may embody that element to a greater degree than all the other elements. You might find that, in general, you embody all the positive attributes of that element. You might also feel that when you are out of balance you express some of the more negative attributes of that element, too.

However, if you scored **within one point on two elements**, you share two dominant elements in combination. For an example, you might be AIR/EARTH dominant or FIRE/WATER dominant.

What if you scored **almost evenly between all the elements**? This means that you have quite a balanced spread of elements, at this time. You may still have a slight preference for one element, but you will find you have little need to seek a particular balancing element to heal an elemental deficiency.

If you scored **particularly low on one element**, however, consider that element your "shadow element" or the element you have developed the least. Pay attention to this element, for it may be the one that offers you the most opportunity for growth.

embarking on your 40-day & 40-night elemental healing journey

You can use this book to learn more about your dominant element/s as well as discovering how the other elements can help create more balance and harmony in your life. There is a section on each of the four elements, which highlights the typical traits of people who are dominated by that particular element and offers advice on how that element can be brought into balance within you, as well as suggesting powerful places you may like to visit to connect with the essence of that element's energy.

This is followed by a powerful guidance section, which outlines a 40-day and 40-night process to help you balance and integrate each element. It is said that within 40 days and 40 nights profound change can be enacted and manifested – you will transform in this short time. At the end of the book, you'll also find a chart summarising some of the traditional correspondences for the four elements as a quick reference guide for further ritual work.

This kit also includes two accompanying guided meditation CDs. Meditation is a powerful way to integrate each element into your life, in a more balanced and deeply transformational way. Please do not worry if you have no experience meditating. Guided meditations offer us a multi-layered experience where our conscious and unconscious minds can relax and yet, learn powerfully at the same time. It's simple: all you need do is get comfortable, free yourself from any potential distractions (for example by leaving your phone in another room), and just listen, relax and allow. The meditations I have created for you are designed to act as a kind of invocation, a primary call towards the energy of the element they relate to, so that energy can be used to bring about healing and inspiration within you. You will feel different after listening, and you'll know the energy of the element is doing its fine work.

There are two main ways to work with the 40-day & 40-night elemental healing journey: a single element option and a four-element option.

SINGLE ELEMENT 40-DAY & 40-NIGHT HEALING JOURNEY

You may choose to dedicate your 40-day process entirely to your dominant element, your 'shadow element', or any element that you feel drawn to work with. In the affirmations sections that follow the information about each element, you'll find pieces of guidance which flow from the deep-seated power of each individual element. These are designed to be considered, meditated on and absorbed one day at a time – there is one for each day in your 40-day process. Select the element you are going to be working with, and feel free to read through all 40 of the affirmations in one go at first, to get a feel for the messages as a whole. Then, at the beginning of your journey, start with the first one on the first day and give it your clear focus for that entire day. Every day, let the messages and images work their magic upon and within you. Every day, you will change and transform.

During the 40-days, listen to the elemental guided meditation for your selected element as many times as you wish – preferably a minimum of once every 10 days, for a total of four times during the 40 days. There will be a new moon during that 40 days, so please, if you can, listen to the meditation that night for extra power. Your mind, body and spirit will integrate this new energy and you'll feel more balanced, joyful and resourceful. Combined with the beautiful and purposeful daily affirmations, you'll find a new, more powerful you is revealed.

FOUR-ELEMENT 40-DAY & 40-NIGHT HEALING JOURNEY

You might like to dedicate your healing journey to all four elements – Earth, Air, Fire and Water. In this case, you'll choose a selection of affirmations from each elemental section while also working with the four guided meditations in this kit.

Days 1-10: Start with your dominant element. Begin each day by selecting one of the 40 affirmations in the section on your dominant element and give it your focus for the whole day. During this 10-day period, make time to listen to the guided meditation track for your dominant element at least three times – or even more if you choose! The idea is to really immerse yourself in the energy of each element and allow the energy to integrate itself within you.

Days 11-20: Move on to your 'shadow' or least dominant element. Start each day by selecting one of the 40 affirmations in the section on your shadow element (you can do them in order or just randomly choose) and give it your focus for the whole day. During this 10-day period, take the time to listen to the guided meditation track for your shadow element at least three times – or even more if you choose! Whilst you might feel challenged playing with this, your least dominant element, please stick with it. Allow the balance and wholeness to begin and feel the difference!

Days 21-30: Select one of the two elements you haven't yet worked with during this process. Begin each day by selecting one of the 40 affirmations in the section on this element and give it your focus for the whole day. During this 10-day period, make time to listen to the guided meditation track for the element at least three times.

Days 31-40: There's one element left! Start each day by selecting one of the 40 affirmations in the section on the element that you have not yet worked with during this journey. Give the affirmation your focus for the whole day. During this 10-day period, take the time to listen to the guided meditation track for this final element at least three times.

To complete the journey in the most balanced way possible, it's a good idea to listen to make time towards the end of the 40 days to complete each of the four guided meditations one more time. On the CDs, you'll notice a 'guided relaxation' track that is repeated before each elemental guided meditation begins. This track is designed to help you relax and prepare yourself for meditation.

Through these guided elemental meditations, your mind, body and spirit will integrate this new energy and you'll feel more balanced, joyful and resourceful. Combined with the beautiful and purposeful daily affirmations, you'll find a new, more powerful you is revealed. Each and every day, you'll build more resilience and you'll find aspects of life that may have felt difficult before, become easier and less stressful. After completing your 40-day and 40-night journey, you'll recognise the elements strongly within you, and you'll be able to use them more readily as powerful tools for self-realisation, renewal and personal power. Remember: you have power! It is real.

earth

The clearest way into the Universe is through a forest wilderness.

– John Muir

about earth element people

It's easy to spot a typical Earth person – they have to spend time outside amongst the green of nature! In fact, in my workshops, we call this urge the need to go "into the big green room." Earth people find peace and renewal in nature. To be at their best in body, mind and spirit, Earth people should spend time outside, in nature or with animals. For instance, the partner that sits outside in the garden after work, with a drink and something nice to snack on? The person that loves their animals as much as they do their people? The sister that gets more excited about growing her own food than most women do about diamonds? The husband that always chooses a camping trip rather than a weekend in the busy concrete jungle of the city? These people are most likely Earth element dominant.

There are other attributes, too, which may not be as easy to spot, but which relate to the very nature of the substance that is earth. For instance, Earth dominant people are typically reliable, solid and secure. In fact, groundedness may be their trademark. This is not to say they are dull or boring. Certainly not! There are many Earth people who are the life of the party – but that party will most often be at their home, where they will present a spread of delicious food and possibly wine they have harvested themselves. They are typically great hosts, and their homes are often simple but beautiful.

As earth is considered one of the "heavier" elements, those with a strong Earth element tend to be deep thinkers, who take time to consider things. So do not try to rush an Earth person into anything! When in balance, however they understand that there is a time and a place for everything and do not allow tasks, burdens, or decisions to add up.

Earth people are typically kind and considerate to others, and are generous with their time. While stereotypes may represent them as staid, they are not particularly conservative. Like the forests, they are growth orientated and love variety. They are often prosperous people who care about the fertility of their bank accounts.

Below, you'll find both the positive and the challenging characteristics of the Earth dominant person. Whether they demonstrate more of the positive or more of the unbalanced traits depends on the balance of earth energy in their current make-up.

the balanced earth element dominant person

Typically, those that embody a high Earth element demonstrate the following positive attributes. They will tend to be

- quite grounded.
- honest and trustworthy.
- sensual, enjoying all the senses, but especially those of taste and touch.
- good in a crisis.
- thoughtful when making decisions.
- slow to anger.
- likely to create a home that is both an emotional and a physical sanctuary.
- open to new ideas.
- prosperous.

- happy to cook, especially for friends and family.
- wonderful hosts, opening their home as a meeting place for friends.
- deeply caring of family and friends; providing for them is a priority.
- typically wonderful gardeners and enjoy growing their own food.
- animal lovers, who almost always invite animals into their spaces.
- able to find refreshment, even after a hard day, by simply sitting on the ground.
- able to cope with hierarchical environments better than most.
- resilient.
- able to work with many kinds of people successfully.
- comfortable with gradual change and will seek growth experiences.
- patient.
- appreciative of simplicity.
- calm in challenging circumstances.
- deep thinkers with good imaginations.
- strong physically and in possession of good stamina.

the out-of-balance earth element dominant person

When out of balance, those that embody a high Earth element may demonstrate the following challenging attributes. They might tend to be:

- stubborn and inflexible.
- ungrounded under severe stress.

- slow to make decisions, at the risk of missing opportunities.
- considered "heavy" and negative by others.
- having trouble sleeping, if anxious.
- stingy with money.
- impatient.
- slow to anger, but then explode.
- stagnant – and aggressive in defending their right not to grow.
- unwilling to release a grudge or to let go of burdens that are not theirs.
- resistant to change.
- highly judgmental and conservative.
- overweight or tending to emotionally overeat.

what earth element people say

These are the kind of comments you might hear from a person with a typically strong Earth element.

"I feel so ungrounded. Everything is happening a bit quickly for me right now."

"This has been fun, but I'm looking forward to spending some quality time at home."

"We are going camping in the holidays."

"Let us go and sit in the park for lunch and get out of the office!"

"I've considered this issue for some time."

"I love to cook. Let me cook for you at my house."

"I feel so peaceful when I can get out into the bush. No phones ringing or people yelling in my ear."

'Trusting someone is very important to me."

"I have invested my money in real estate."

"There is nothing like walking in nature. Every step energises me."

"I find that person hard to relate to. They are so aggressive, and what they say isn't really rational."

"Let me help you work through this. I understand that it's difficult."

"I put up with this for a long time, and then enough was enough, and I really got very angry."

lacking in earth element?

If you scored particularly low on the Earth element, it may be your "shadow element" or the element you have developed the least. Interestingly, this may be the element that offers you the most opportunity for growth.

Why would you wish to balance yourself with more of the Earth element?

After all, you might not particularly like the idea of Earth energy. Yet, if we are going to be more rounded and whole as people, developing an element we don't naturally favour can bring us a greater sense of balance and strength – which, in turn, can help us have a better life.

what the earth element can offer to other elements

Water Element: If you are Water element dominant, you may find that when you are out of balance you lose focus or have a tendency to be "wishy-washy" and emotionally indecisive. In this case, bringing in more of the wise groundedness of Earth may help you feel more centred and sure of yourself again.

Fire Element: If you are Fire element dominant, you may find that when you are out of balance you tend to be overly enthusiastic or to make decisions too quickly. In this case, bringing in some of the slower, more deliberate energy of Earth may help you regain your stability and be able to more easily wisely consider longer-term concerns.

Air Element: If you are Air element dominant, you may find that when you are out of balance, it is difficult to focus on one thing, or you struggle to act on solutions that require a long-term approach. In this case, Earth's rational, calm properties may help ground your thinking so you can take step-by-step action, over time, to make your dreams a reality.

earth element power spots

It might be obvious to suggest that people who have a strong Earth element give themselves the opportunity to spend time in natural environments on a regular basis. However, it is surprising how many Earth people either do not recognise their need for this or do not take the initiative to make sure they do so.

To be at your best, if you are Earth element dominant, spending time within your physical element – nature – is vital to your wellbeing. In fact, I believe that Earth folk, as well as those who identify strongly with Water, require regular immersion in their element. Balance for you means experiencing your element physically, not just thinking about or imagining it. You must actually step forth into your green sanctuary!

There are special places on earth where we can plug into our dominant element and where particular elements are exceptionally powerful. The ancients were aware of such places and often built temples or other religious structures on these special places of power.

For the Earth element, these sacred places have extraordinary resonance:

- Göbekli Tepe (Turkey)
- The Fairy Circles (Namibia)

- Avebury Standing Stones (United Kingdom)
- Machu Picchu (Peru)
- Ajanta Caves (India)
- The Magnetic North and South Poles
- Mnajdra Temples (Malta)
- Uluru (Australia)
- Maasai Mara (Kenya)
- The Obsidian Walls in Yellowstone National Park (USA)
- Taormina (Sicily)
- Volubilis (Morocco)

If you wish to read about these places, the energies they hold and how they might help you, you can learn more in my oracle deck *Earth Power: An Atlas for the Soul*.

the guidance

It is said that within 40 days and 40 nights profound change can be enacted and manifested. The following pieces of guidance flow from the deep-seated power of Earth. They are designed to be considered, meditated on and absorbed one day at a time. Feel free to read through the entire section first, to get a feel for the messages as a whole. Then begin at the beginning, and give each one your focus, in turn, for a single day. Every day, let the messages work their magic upon and within you. Every day, you will change.

Receive.

40 days & 40 nights
of guidance
from the element
of earth

1. MOTHER EARTH CRADLES ME FROM THE MOMENT I AM BORN.

2. I AM CONNECTED TO ALL.

3. I AM PART OF THE INTERCONNECTEDNESS OF THE EARTH AND ALL THE ENERGY SHE OFFERS.

4. LISTEN TO THE HEARTBEAT OF THE PLANET.

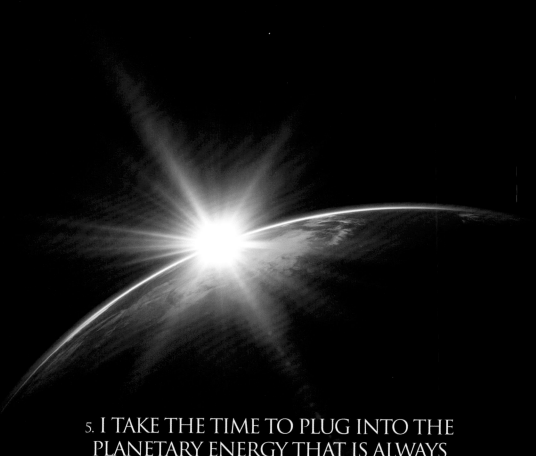

5. I TAKE THE TIME TO PLUG INTO THE PLANETARY ENERGY THAT IS ALWAYS WAITING FOR ME.

6. I AWAKEN AND GIVE THANKS FOR EVERY DAY AND EVERY GIFT I AM GIVEN.

7. BEFORE
I SLEEP,
I AM
GRATEFUL
FOR THE
DARK
AND
RESTFUL
NIGHT.

8. THE EARTH PROVIDES ME WITH SO MUCH; I AM AWARE OF THE PRINCIPLES OF RECIPROCITY.

9. I TAKE THE TIME
TO BE GRATEFUL FOR
ALL OF MY SENSES.

10. MY FOOD IS NOURISHING, ALIVE AND
AS CLEAN AS POSSIBLE; I AM AWARE OF
ITS SOURCES.

11. LIKE THE ROOTS OF A TREE SEEKING THE EARTH, I GROUND FIRMLY AND EASILY.

12. WHILST FULLY GROUNDED, I AM STILL FLEXIBLE AND OPEN TO NEW EXPERIENCES.

13. I AM OPEN AND RESPONSIVE
TO THE NOURISHMENT AND
ABUNDANCE OF THE UNIVERSE.

14. I WALK INTO THE "BIG GREEN ROOM OF NATURE" AND I AM CALMED.

15. PEACE IS AVAILABLE TO ME AT EVERY MOMENT.

16. FROM A PLACE OF
PEACEFUL SUPPORT,
I CAN PLAN MY
JOURNEY TO THE
STARS.

17. I DO NOT FEAR GROWTH, JUST AS THE
BUD IS NOT AFRAID TO FLOWER.

18. I FOLLOW THE EARTH'S SEASONAL CYCLES FOR A FLOW OF HEALTH AND BALANCE.

19. EVERY FOOTSTEP ON THE EARTH BRINGS ME MORE JOY AND PURPOSE.

20. EVERY FOOTSTEP BRINGS ME CLOSER TO THE LIFE EXPERIENCES THAT I WANT.

21. I AM UNAFRAID
TO TAKE RISKS.

22. I KNOW THAT IF I PLANT SEEDS – IDEAS, NEW BEGINNINGS, GOOD WORKS – THEY WILL GROW.

23. I AM NOT AFRAID TO THINK BIG AND
SET LONG-TERM GOALS.

24. I MOVE WITH GRACE, LIGHTNESS AND FLOW.

25. I AM SOUL-CENTRED FROM THE INSIDE OUT.

26. I CHOOSE TO LET GO OF INAPPROPRIATE BURDENS. I RETURN BURDENS THAT ARE NOT MINE.

27. I PRUNE BACK ANYTHING WITHIN ME
THAT IS OUT OF BALANCE.

28. I KNOW THAT RESISTING CHANGE IS RESISTING NATURE. THEREFORE, I WELCOME CHANGE.

29. THERE IS A SEASON FOR EVERYTHING, AND ALL SEASONS GIVE WAY TO THE NEXT.

30. I BLOOM AND BLOSSOM TOWARDS
MY GREATEST POTENTIAL.

31. THE FALLOW FIELD IS NOT EMPTY. IT IS FULL OF POSSIBILITY.

32. I CAN CREATE WHAT I WANT AT WILL, JUST AS IF I WERE MODELLING WITH CLAY.

33. I AM PURPOSEFUL,
YES, AND I AM ALSO
PREPARED TO WALK
OFF THE PATH AT TIMES.

34. I AM EXPANSIVE.

35. I DISSOLVE MY ANXIETY
IN A MILLION SHADES OF GREEN.

36. I UNFURL MY LOVE AND DESIRE LIKE A TENDER NEW LEAF.

37. I BUILD A WEB TO CONNECT ALL BEINGS ON THE PLANET, FOR THE GREATER GOOD.

38. I CAN BE BOTH THE SALT OF THE EARTH AND, AS WELL, THE SUNLIGHT THROUGH THE TREES.

39. I AM LOVED
AND SUPPORTED.

40. THE EARTH IS AN AMAZING PLACE, IF I CHOOSE TO LOOK. IT IS MY HOME AND MY SANCTUARY.

air

The mountains are calling and I must go.

– John Muir

about air element people

While the term "air head" refers to a person who is scatterbrained, those with a dominant Air element are actually excellent thinkers and communicators. Their currency in trade is ideas, and getting ideas across is their greatest strength. Air people naturally gravitate to wide open spaces. They are at their best when they have regular opportunities to get outside, feel the wind on their skin and breathe the fresh air, which helps them to "clear their heads."

The genius inventor that never runs out of ideas? The writer that creates whole worlds in her head? The friend that delights in the vista from the top of a mountain? The sister who runs out into a storm and loves getting the wild wind in her hair? The person with the melodious voice and great orating style? All are most likely Air element dominant.

There are other attributes, too, that may not be as easy to spot, but which relate to the nature of air. For instance, Air dominant people value creating something from nothing and gain energy from sharing their ideas and words. They value freedom and autonomy highly and enjoy having room to create, to think, to move and to play. Many entrepreneurs are Air Element dominant.

As air governs the breath and all forms of communication, Air people revel in being efficient, effective communicators and often work as writers, bloggers, coaches, teachers and filmmakers. Their rational and dispassionate nature also suits them for work in the sciences. They are good planners and strategists. They also love fragrance, so may be perfumers.

Great working partnerships are often formed between Air and Fire (air feeds fire) where the Air person communicates and directs the activities and passion of the Fire person. (For example, when a focused activist or politician needs a great strategist or communicator to get their ideas across).

Generally, Air people are quick and deep thinking. They can be interested in what makes people tick, but may lack empathy. Also, they may simply leave if challenged too often or restrained too long, as they tend to become depressed if their freedom is jeopardised. In the workplace, should they be over-managed, they grow unhappy quickly. They are often puzzled about displays of dramatic emotion, but, like Water people, forgive readily without holding a grudge.

Below, you'll find both the positive and the challenging characteristics of the Air dominant person. Whether they demonstrate more of the positive or more of the challenging traits depends on the balance of air energy in their current make-up.

the balanced air element dominant person

Typically, those who embody a high Air element demonstrate the following positive attributes. They will tend to be:

- highly capable and mentally flexible.
- aware of their skill in communicating well to a variety of people.
- quite strategic; they enjoy doing their research.
- very curious.
- good at mental gymnastics and games .
- often funny.

- sensitive to smells.
- rational and thoughtful about different points of view.
- willing to let go and move on after conflict.
- adventurous; they most likely love travel.
- able to get over crisis quickly.
- appreciative of "weather", especially storms and wind.
- happy at high altitudes, like on mountains or in skyscrapers (they would enjoy flying in aeroplanes more if the space was less restrictive).
- adaptable, but unhappy if micromanaged or restricted in their creativity.
- strong problem solvers.
- able to take advantage of opportunities when they arise.
- quick thinking.
- lithe, with a good energy level.

the out-of-balance air element dominant person

When out of balance, those that embody a high Air element may demonstrate the following challenging attributes. They might tend to be:

- forgetful or confused.
- overly detached; uninterested others' points of view.
- seen as cold and unemotional by others.
- ungrounded in their actions and views.
- focused on escaping, literally or mentally, instead of on facing issues.

- unfocused and lose motivation.
- manipulative rather than strategic.
- wary and distrustful of people.
- controlling of others to keep to their plans.
- susceptible to procrastination or writer's block.
- susceptible to weight loss if overly anxious; they may also lose their voice.
- agoraphobic or claustrophobic.
- focused on the mind to the detriment of the body.

what air element people say

These are the kind of comments you might hear from a person with a typically strong Air element.

"Last night I watched the most amazing storm come in. It almost blew my hair straight off my head. It was so cool!"

"I got lost in that book."

"I've booked a ski holiday in a mountain resort. The views are incredible."

"Why were they so emotional about that movie? It wasn't real!"

"Mmm, can you smell that?" (No, often you can't! Only the Air person can!)

"Let's try it this way; we haven't tried that before."

"If I don't get out of this office at lunch time, I'm going to kill someone."

"Let's get out of here; I need some air."

"I've got a great idea – and then another one!"

"I'm quitting because my boss continually micromanages me."

"I want a higher perspective on this, as I don't want to get bogged down."

"I'm happy I understand the reasons she chose the way she did."

"I find him hard to relate to. He is so dramatic and emotional."

"I understand why you got upset. I don't hold grudges, so let's work it through."

lacking in air element?

If you scored particularly low on the Air element, it may be your "shadow element" or the element you have developed the least. Interestingly, this may be the element that offers you the most opportunity for growth.

Why would you wish to balance yourself with more of the Air element?

After all, you might not particularly like the idea of Air energy. Yet, if we are going to be more rounded and whole as people, developing an element we don't naturally favour can bring us a greater sense of balance and strength – which, in turn, can help us have a better life.

what the air element can offer to other elements

Earth Element: If you are Earth element dominant, you may find that when you are out of balance you have a tendency to be inflexible or overly serious. In this case, Air's quick responsiveness and playfulness may help lighten your mood and bring you a sense of freedom and new possibilities.

Fire Element: If you are Fire element dominant, you may find that when you are out of balance you become either autocratic or impulsive. In this case, Air's ability to create practical strategies and communicate those strategies in a diplomatic way may help you accomplish what you want – while maintaining the support of those you value. Air and fire can be a powerful combination if utilised well.

Water Element: If you are Water element dominant, you may find that when you are out of balance, you have a tendency to lose your motivation and will, and simply "dissolve" – or alternatively, become overwhelmed by emotion. The buoyancy of Air can lift you free of any emotional "undertow", while Air's fresh breeze can refill your sails and get you moving again.

air element power spots

It might be obvious to suggest that people who have a strong Air element give themselves the opportunity to spend time near high places or in places that are very open on a regular basis. However, it is surprising how many Air people either do not recognise their need for this or do not take the initiative to make sure they do so.

To be at your best, if you are Air element dominant, spending time within your physical element is vital to your wellbeing. Try to find places that are not crowded, where the wind is literally in your hair. Watch clouds go by, birds soaring and storms brewing! You might also find practices which focus on the breath, for example pranayama and yoga, are also beneficial to your wellbeing.

There are special places on earth where we can plug into our dominant element and where particular elements are exceptionally powerful. The ancients were aware of such places and often built temples or other religious structures on these special places of power.

For the Air element, these sacred places have extraordinary resonance:

- Mount Kailash (Tibet)
- Mount Everest (Nepal and India)
- Machu Picchu (Peru)
- Glastonbury Tor (England)
- Mecca (Saudi Arabia)
- Delphi (Greece)
- Cathedral of Notre Dame (France)

- The Statue of Liberty (USA)
- Svalbard (between Norway and the Arctic)

If you wish to read about these places, the energies they hold and how they might help you, you can learn more in my oracle deck *Earth Power: An Atlas for the Soul.*

the guidance

It is said that within 40 days and 40 nights profound change can be enacted and manifested. The following pieces of guidance flow from the deep-seated power of Air. They are designed to be considered, meditated on and absorbed one day at a time. Feel free to read through the entire section first, to get a feel for the messages as a whole. Then begin at the beginning, and give each one your focus, in turn, for a single day. Every day, let the messages work their magic upon and within you. Every day, you will change.

Receive.

40 days & 40 nights
of guidance
from the element
of air

1. BREATHE…

2. BREATHE IN THE POWER OF THE UNIVERSE AND THE DELIGHT OF ALL THINGS.

3. BREATHE OUT WHAT YOU NEED TO HOLD NO LONGER.

4. I ALLOW THE WIND TO
PLAY UPON MY SKIN,
FEELING EVERY CARESS.

5. I TASTE THE AIR
AND LIFT MY FACE
TO SMELL THE BREEZE.

6. FRAGRANCES
ARE STORIES IN
THE AIR.

7. THERE IS AN EASE AND FREEDOM
IN EVERYTHING I DO.

8. I AM CONNECTED:
I CAN BE EVERYWHERE,
AT ANY TIME.

9. LIKE A BIRD ON A THERMAL,
I AM SUPPORTED,
AS A CHILD OF THE UNIVERSE

10. I ALLOW WHAT IS NOT MINE TO SIMPLY BE RELEASED AND FLOAT AWAY.

11. I CAN MOVE AND CHOOSE
WITH EASE AND GRACE.

12. EVEN THE
MOST INTENSE
STORM PASSES.

13. I SPEAK MY
WORD WITH
OPENNESS
AND CLARITY.

14. MY VOICE IS PURPOSEFUL
AND MUSICAL.

15. MY
COMMUNICATION
WITH OTHERS
IS FULL OF LOVE,
INTELLIGENCE AND
PURPOSE.

16. I CHOOSE MY OWN FUTURE. EVERY DECISION I MAKE BRINGS ME CLOSER TO WHO I REALLY AM AND THE LIFE I WISH TO LIVE.

17. MY HEART, BODY AND MIND ARE IN UNISON.

18. I FEEL BOTH FREE
AND GROUNDED
AT THE SAME TIME.

19. I HAVE
PERSPECTIVE
IN DIFFICULT
CIRCUMSTANCES.

20. I RISE ABOVE LOWER ENERGIES.

21. I CAN BE STILL.
I CAN HOVER
IN PERFECT BALANCE.

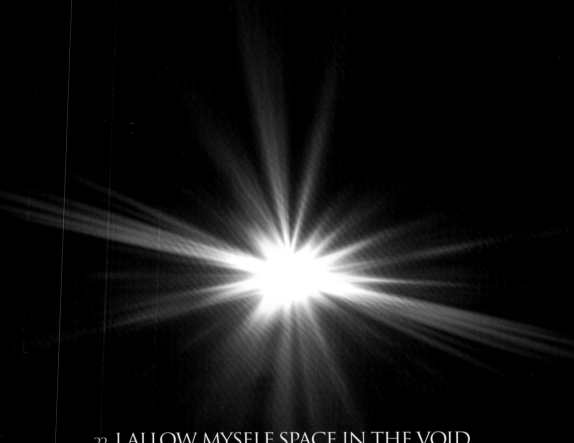

22. I ALLOW MYSELF SPACE IN THE VOID.
I LISTEN – AND HEAR MUCH WITHIN
THE SILENCE.

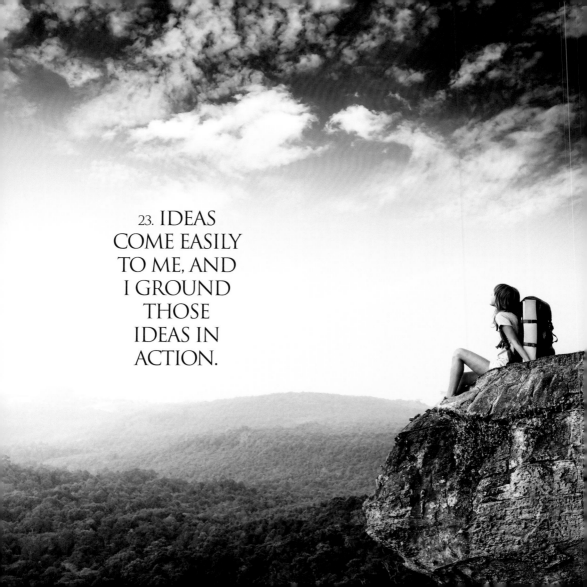

23. IDEAS COME EASILY TO ME, AND I GROUND THOSE IDEAS IN ACTION.

24. I AM TRUSTWORTHY AND DO NOT ENGAGE IN GOSSIP.

25. I USE MY INTELLECT FOR BOTH THE GREATER GOOD AND MY OWN GOOD.

26. LAUGHTER RINGS THROUGH MY
BODY AND SOUL, LIGHTENING AND
ENLIGHTENING.

27. I HAVE FAITH THAT ALL WILL BE WELL, EVEN IF I ENCOUNTER OBSTACLES.

28. I AM COMPLETELY CENTRED AND SECURE.

29. I TAKE
A LEAP OF
FAITH.

30. WITHOUT FEAR I CAN DECIDE TO DEEPLY CONNECT TO SOMEONE OR SOMETHING.

31. I WELCOME THE SACRED MYSTERY INTO MY LIFE. I DON'T HAVE TO KNOW EVERYTHING.

32. MY SOUL IS "LIGHT-HEARTED", SO MY WORRIES ARE AS LIGHT AS A FEATHER.

33. I ENJOY MOVING MY BODY AND CHALLENGING MY MIND.

34. LIKE MUSIC,
MY LOVE PULSES
THROUGH
WHAT IS RIGID
AND HARSH.

35. I DREAM AND
ENJOY THE
SENSATION OF
FREE-FLOWING
IMAGINATION.

36. I AM BOTH DELICIOUSLY CREATIVE AND BEAUTIFULLY PRACTICAL.

37. I CAN SOAR
ABOVE THE ORDINARY.

38. WHEN I FOCUS MY ENERGY, I CAN ACHIEVE ANYTHING I CHOOSE.

39. I AM INDEPENDENT,
AND YET I HAVE DEEP AND LASTING
RELATIONSHIPS OF ALL KINDS.

40. THE SOURCE OF ALL CONNECTION IS MY BREATH. I BREATHE, AND ALL I NEED IS THERE.

fire

*Love is a fire. But whether its going to warm your hearth
or burn down your house, you never can tell.*

– Joan Crawford

about fire element people

We all recognise Fire people. They are the fast ones that make things happen. Their unbridled passion for whatever they are interested in makes them stand out. You'll find Fire people anywhere change is happening. They are natural leaders, who inspire others to come along with them on the journey or join forces with them for the mission. Heads of businesses, activists, producers, athletes, military leaders, if someone needs to hold their energy and lead others, they usually have strong Fire tendencies.

Fire people are absolutely passionate when in love, too. They are sensual; they sweep people off their feet and will tell the object of their affection, without hesitation, how they feel when they are besotted. They are powerful persuaders and can be quite wilful in nature. But if something goes wrong, they are quick to recover and move on – happily leaving bridges burning behind if it suits them.

Fire people are also innovators and artists, and they are courageous, risk taking and have high levels of physical energy – which can, at times, lead to burn out.

The friend that is endlessly stimulated by the new gadgets? The brother that is totally, passionately in love with his new girlfriend and never stops talking about her? The artist that works all day and night until her work is finished? The unstoppable force who changes the law? These are most likely Fire element dominant.

Fire is considered one of the action orientated, lighter elements. Therefore, those with a strong Fire element tend to be quick thinkers who transform thought into action just as rapidly as they conceive it. They share this tendency with Air people, whose element is also considered lighter and action oriented.

Put an obstacle in front of a Fire person, and they will do everything in their means to burn that obstacle to a crisp in a hurry!

They often volunteer, giving generously of their time and considerable energy. They make for great mentors, and act as a lighthouse for others, sending out a guiding beam via their positive work ethic and enthusiasm. They are often quite successful in their chosen field, but may be considered difficult to work with if they do not temper their hot, hot flame!

Below, you'll find both the positive and the challenging characteristics of the Fire dominant person. Whether they demonstrate more of the positive or more of the challenging traits depends on the balance of fire energy in their current make-up.

the balanced fire element dominant person

Typically, those who embody a high Fire element demonstrate the following positive attributes. They will tend to be:

- passionate, with a healthy drive.
- quick thinkers who process information quickly.
- able and willing to express emotions fully.
- action-orientated.
- quick to process emotions.
- catalysts who actually make change happen.
- innovative and open to new ideas.

- focused and single-minded; they love being totally absorbed in a project.
- stimulated and motivated by crowds and group energy.
- very intuitive.
- high achievers.
- artistic and creative.
- inspirational, often leaders.
- passionate lovers.
- romantic and charismatic.
- early adopters of technology.
- quite physical, enjoying exercise and movement.
- dynamic.
- enthusiastic and easily excited.
- willing to burn a bridge, and to do so with gusto.
- able to juggle more than one thing at once.
- good at competitive sports – especially those that require bursts of energy.
- great fun to be around, with a quick sense of humour.

the out-of-balance fire element dominant person

When out of balance, those who embody a high Fire element may demonstrate the following challenging attributes. They might tend to be:

- pushy, wilful and aggressive.
- too quick to make decisions.

- manipulative of others' emotions.
- inconsiderate of others' time, considering only their own timetable.
- destructive.
- passionate in their hatred.
- extremely impatient.
- quick to anger; this can escalate to rage, tantrums or even violence.
- vain, proud and revenge-seeking.
- overly competitive.
- overly social, partying too hard.
- at risk of burn out.
- too reliant on short cuts, or acting without due diligence.
- underweight or at risk of drug addiction.

what fire element people say

These are the kind of comments you might hear from a person with a typically strong Fire element.

"I feel so excited about this project. I cannot wait to start."

"There is a festival on. Three days! Let's party!"

"This needs to change, and change now!"

"I've decided. Next issue?"

"Let's get this done."

"How fast can we get this done?"

"I love this new idea. It lights me up."

"I'm so passionate about this!"

"I've never felt like this before. It's so intense!"

"What do you mean it's too hot? It's perfect!"

"I find him hard to relate to. He is so slow at getting things done and has no focus."

"Let me help you work through this. I've done this before and can show you how."

"I put up with it for a little while, but enough is enough! I got very angry."

lacking in fire element?

If you scored particularly low on the Fire element, it may be your "shadow element" or the element you have developed the least. Interestingly, this may be the element that offers you the most opportunity for growth.

Why would you wish to balance yourself with more of the Fire element?

After all, you might not particularly like the idea of Fire energy. Yet, if we are going to be more rounded and whole as people, developing an element we don't naturally favour can bring us a greater sense of balance and strength – which, in turn, can help us have a better life.

what the fire element can offer to other elements

Water Element: If you are Water element dominant, you may find that when you are out of balance you have a tendency to be overwhelmed, unfocused or insecure – any of which can keep you from supporting others and continuing ahead with your life's purpose. In this case, bringing in the quick clarity and confidence of fire – not to mention its action-oriented energy – may help remove the clouds of emotion from your perceptions and support you in regaining the self trust necessary to move forward.

Earth Element: If you are Earth element dominant, you might find that when you are out of balance you weigh choices for so long you actually lose opportunities. Or your sense of responsibility to others may keep you from acting on your own behalf. Try bringing in fire's quick intuitive wisdom and willingness to consider their own needs. By helping you trust your judgement and prioritise yourself appropriately, fire energy can help you enjoy life again!

Air Element: If you are Air element dominant, you may find that when you are out of balance you create more ideas than you can act on. You may also be so "in your head" that you treat others' feelings with little concern. In this case, try bringing in fire's enthusiasm to make things happen and rekindle your warm passionate nature. You may find your ideas are even better when you put them to use and your relationships more productive when you show sympathy to those around you. Generally, Air people work well alongside Fire people, as they feed each other's strengths and strengthen each other's weak points.

fire element power spots

It might be obvious to suggest that people who have a strong Fire element give themselves the opportunity to spend time in warmer or more active environments on a regular basis. However, it is surprising how many Fire people either do not recognise their need for this or do not take the initiative to make sure they do so.

To be at your best, if you are Fire element dominant, you'll need to spend time in environments that stimulate you. This may be a city, where Fire people do very well, as they thrive on the hustle and bustle. But Fire people can actually thrive in almost any dynamic work situation. For instance, many artists are Fire people. They are creative, expressive and full of passion for their art. Wherever they can completely focus on creating their work is a great environment for them. But keeping a Fire person from the stimulation and inspiration that feeds them is tantamount to starving them. Fire people must be focused and have a purpose.

There are special places on earth where we can plug into our element and where particular elements are inordinately more powerful. The ancients were very aware of such places and often built temples or other religious structures on these special places of power.

For the Fire element, these sacred places have extraordinary resonance:

- Death Valley (USA)
- The Sahara (Africa)
- Valley of the Kings (Egypt)
- Mount Kilauea (Hawaii)
- Mount Etna (Sicily)
- Zoroastrian temple of Pir-e Naraki (Iran)
- Jeshoreshwari Kali Temple (Bangladesh)

If you wish to read about these places, the energies they hold and how they might help you, you can learn more in my oracle deck *Earth Power: An Atlas for the Soul*.

the guidance

It is said that within 40 days and 40 nights profound change can be enacted manifested. The following pieces of guidance flow from the deep-seated power of Fire. They are designed to be considered, meditated on and absorbed one day at a time. However, feel free to read through the entire section first, to get a feel for the messages as a whole. Then begin at the beginning, and give each one your focus, in turn, for a single day. Every day, let the messages work their magic upon and within you. Every day, you will change.

Receive.

40 days & 40 nights
of guidance
from the element
of fire

1. I HAVE AN INFINITE FLAME WITHIN ME.

2. I CONTAIN A GLOW THAT CAN BE
SHARED WITH ALL.

3. I SEE THE RADIANCE
IN EVERYONE
AND EVERYTHING.

4. MY HEART
IS AFLAME
WITH LOVE.

5. I POWERFULLY DANCE
MY WISHES INTO REALITY.

6. I AM ALIVE AND
PASSIONATE ABOUT
MY PURPOSE.

7. I CAN BE DELIGHTED AND
ENTHUSED ABOUT MY FUTURE.

8. I OFFER A BLAZING LIGHT
THAT SHINES FOR THOSE IN DARKNESS.

9. LIKE A CANDLE THAT ILLUMINATES,
I SEE DARKNESS OF ALL KINDS
RECEDING.

10. I AM POWERFUL WHEN I AM AWARE
OF MY EMOTIONS IN REAL TIME.

11. I AM MINDFUL OF
HOW I COMMUNICATE
WITH OTHERS.

12. I FIND BALANCE IN EVERYTHING I DO.

13. I REDUCE TO ASHES
WHAT I NO LONGER NEED.

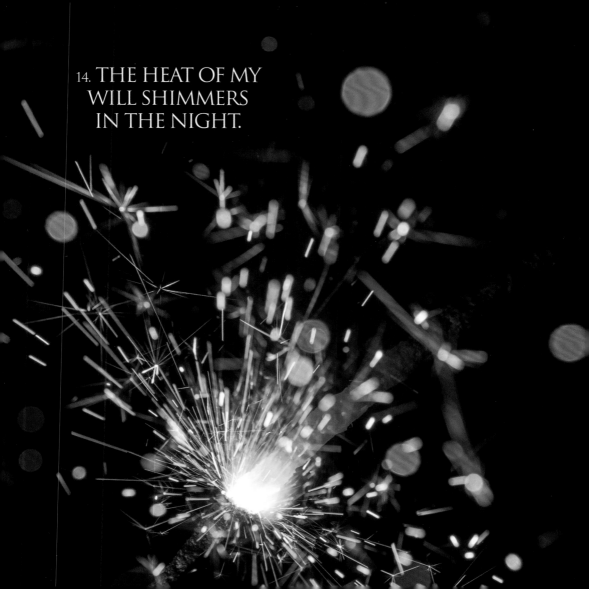

14. THE HEAT OF MY
WILL SHIMMERS
IN THE NIGHT.

15. I NOURISH MYSELF AND OTHERS,

AND TEMPER MY EGO IF NECESSARY.

16. I CHOOSE
TO BE ALL
THAT MY
POTENTIAL
INTENDS ME
TO BE.

17. I AM ABLE TO CHANGE WITHOUT
FEAR OR DESTROYING ALL.

18. I ILLUMINATE MY OWN PATH WITH A TORCH OF TRUTH.

19. THE PLACES THAT I FOCUS MY EFFORT AND ENERGY REVEAL A LOT ABOUT ME.

20. I AM
FULL OF
PULSING
VITALITY.

21. TRANSCENDING INERTIA,
I AM HAPPY AND CONFIDENT
ABOUT THE PATH AHEAD.

22. AT TIMES, I AM OPEN AND RESPONSIVE
TO DEEPER, SLOWER RHYTHMS OF LIFE.

23. I CAN BANK MY PASSION, PRACTICE PATIENCE AND WAIT FOR THE PERFECT TIME.

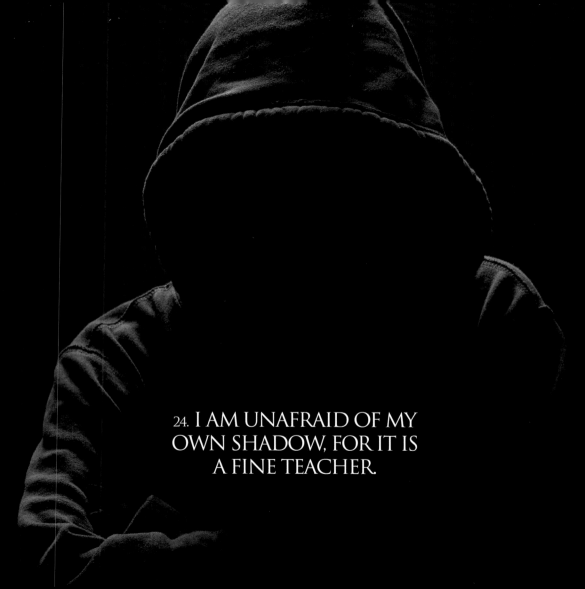

24. I AM UNAFRAID OF MY OWN SHADOW, FOR IT IS A FINE TEACHER.

25. I CAN BRING WARMTH
TO THE COLD-HEARTED.

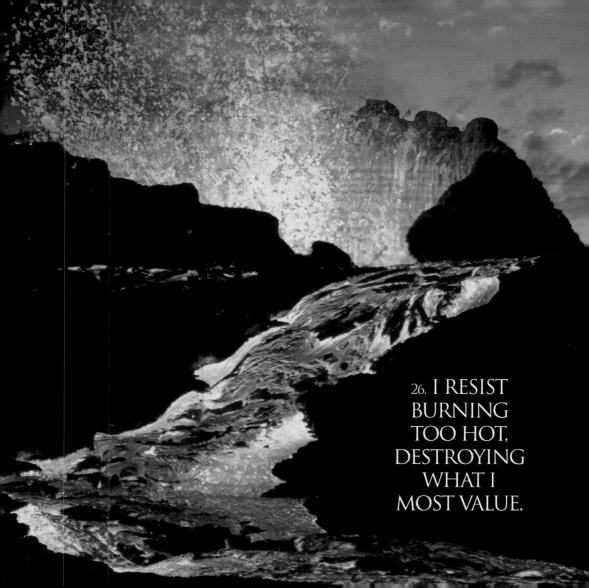

26. I RESIST BURNING TOO HOT, DESTROYING WHAT I MOST VALUE.

27.
BURNING
AWAY
ILLUSION,
I KNOW
MY TRUE
SELF.

28. CLEARING AWAY CLUTTER BRINGS SPACE FOR THE NEW.

29. I SHIMMER WITH COSMIC DELIGHT, LOVING ALL THINGS.

30. THERE IS AN ELECTRIC FORCE WITHIN ME THAT ATTRACTS WHAT I NEED.

31. I ENCOURAGE SPARKS OF
AWE AND WONDER,
NOT SPARKS OF ANGER AND RAGE.

32. I KEEP THE HOME FIRES BURNING
AND HAVE A WARM AND
WELCOMING HOME.

33. I MANAGE MY
PASSIONS EASILY,
ALLOWING THEM TO
EXPAND AND RIPPLE.

34. MY PASSION FOR MY BELOVED CATCHES EVERYTHING ALIGHT!

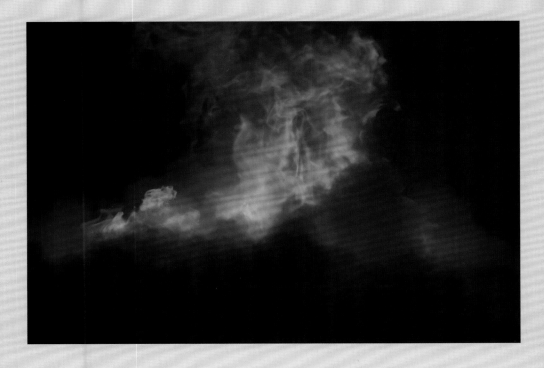

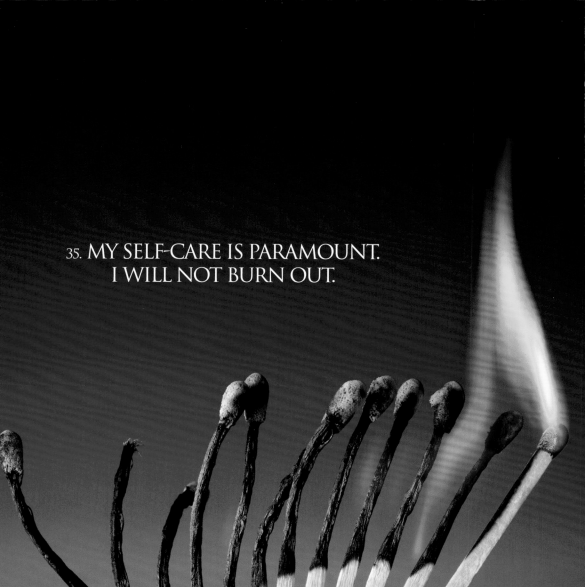

35. MY SELF-CARE IS PARAMOUNT.
I WILL NOT BURN OUT.

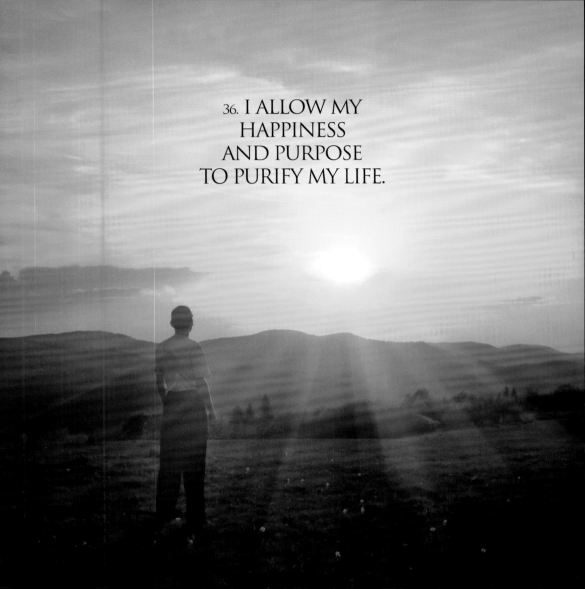

36. I ALLOW MY
HAPPINESS
AND PURPOSE
TO PURIFY MY LIFE.

37. I NEED ONLY RETURN TO THE GENTLE WARMTH WITHIN MY HEART TO FIND A PLACE OF PEACE AND BALANCE.

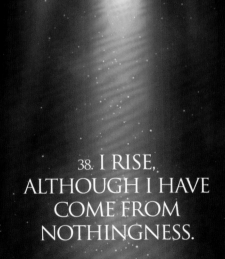

38. I RISE,
ALTHOUGH I HAVE
COME FROM
NOTHINGNESS.

39. I AM GRATEFUL FOR EVERY DAY I AM ALIVE. AT DAWN, I GIVE THANKS. AT SUNSET, I GIVE THANKS.

40. I AM A BEING OF LUMINOSITY,
A LIVING EXPRESSION OF
THE LIGHT OF THE SOURCE.

water

My soul is full of longing for the secret of the sea,
and the heart of the great ocean sends a thrilling pulse through me.

– Henry Wordsworth Longfellow

about water element people

Water people are some of the easiest to spot among the "Big Four." They naturally gravitate to water and are at their best when they have a regular water touchstone. No matter whether it is a natural body of water or man-made, Water people find peace and renewal near water.

To be at their best in body, mind and spirit, Water people should spend time by rivers, lakes, and the ocean. They do well to take up swimming or kayaking or other activities that bring them to their favourite element on a regular basis. So, the partner that loses hours surfing – and has a quiver of boards to be able to take advantage of every size of wave? The friend that saved for years to buy a shack by the ocean? The cousin that swims for hours, chasing the line on the pool bottom? The brother who would live underwater if he could? They are most likely Water element people, who need to spend time by or on or in the water to meet their elemental needs.

There are other attributes, too, which may not be as easy to spot, but which relate to the very nature of the substance that is water. For instance, Water people are typically quite fluid and flexible, and are often said to "go with the flow." They can also be as changeable as water – smooth and calm one moment and stormy and choppy the next. Likewise, they can be as deep as the sea in their thinking or as shallow as a puddle.

As water governs the emotions in many elemental theories, those with a strong water element are emotional beings, in touch with what they are feeling and, if balanced and healthy, can be very emotionally intelligent. Therefore, many Water people find their calling as therapists or in other roles in which they can use their abilities to understand and support the emotions of others.

They are forward thinking, often quite open, generous, and social. They are quite even tempered and forgive readily, without holding a grudge. At their best, Water people can be a force for change – but their changeable emotions can lead them to be "wishy-washy" when it comes decision-making, if they are not aware enough of their tendencies.

Below, you'll find both the positive and the challenging characteristics of the Water dominant person. Whether they demonstrate more of the positive or more of the challenging traits depends on the balance of water energy in their current make-up.

the balanced water element dominant person

Typically, those who embody a high Water element demonstrate the following positive attributes. They will tend to be:

- highly flexible and resilient.
- aware of their emotions and their cause.
- highly sensual, especially regarding touch and the "feel" of something.
- empathetic.
- able to let go and move on after conflict.
- adventurous and risk taking.
- even tempered.
- attracted to the sea and its creatures, as well as to other bodies of water.
- Often committed to living near water.

- refreshed, even after a hard day, simply by encountering water but especially by being submerged in it.
- very adaptable, but unhappy if contained for a long period of time.
- creative.
- able to take advantage of opportunities when they arise.
- forward thinking and in the flow in their views and ideas.
- calm in challenging circumstances.
- accepting of support and willing to take a leap.
- physically graceful.
- tuned in to others' emotions.
- good listeners.
- friendly, kind and generous.
- easy company to be with.
- highly intuitive.
- lovers of art and appreciative of beauty.

the out-of-balance water element dominant person

When out of balance, those who embody a high Water element may demonstrate the following challenging attributes. They might tend to be:

- indecisive and "wishy-washy" about their opinions.
- overly emotional.

- extremely sensitive to emotional hurts and unable to rationalise.
- seen as moody by others.
- unable to easily find grounding and balance.
- easily addicted, in an attempt to bolster insecurities.
- stagnant about their growth at times; reluctant to "try" any more.
- under motivated.
- easily led by others because they find it simpler to go with the flow.
- physically "soft" and prone to watery conditions like pneumonia, tissue swelling or poor kidney function.
- easily halted on a project, losing confidence and "heart" for it.
- in need of constant reassurance

what water element people say

These are the kind of comments you might hear from a person with a typically strong Water element.

"I was having a tough day. Then I went and washed it all away with a swim."

"A long, hot bath is the best thing ever for relaxation."

"I've booked a cruise for my holiday."

"That movie made me cry. I bawled in the cinema!"

"I feel deeply for that person. I know how they feel."

"If I don't get a surf in, I will explode."

"My dream is to live by the sea."

"My writing just flowed."

"When I swim, the feel of my body moving through the water is amazing."

"I'm so happy I was ready for that opportunity."

"I find that person hard to relate to. She is so inflexible and stuck."

"Thank you for the offer of support. I'll accept that help."

"I was angry, but I don't hold grudges."

lacking in water element?

If you scored particularly low on the Water element, it may be your "shadow element" or the element you have developed the least. Interestingly, this may be the element that offers you the most opportunity for growth.

Why would you wish to balance yourself with more of the Water element?

After all, you might not particularly like the idea of Water energy. Yet, if we are going to be more rounded and whole as people, developing an element we don't naturally favour can bring us a greater sense of balance and strength – which, in turn, can help us have a better life.

what the water element can offer to other elements

Earth Element: If you are Earth element dominant, you may find that when you are out of balance you have a tendency to be inflexible, fixed in your thinking or stuck in a course of action. In this case, bringing in more of the flowing responsiveness of water may help you feel freer to consider – and even adopt – alternative opinions or paths.

Fire Element: If you are Fire element dominant, you may find that when you are out of balance you have a tendency to be overly confident, too forceful or even pushy. In this case, bringing in more of water's free-flowing, accepting nature may help you find greater peace and equanimity, so you can allow events – and people! – to develop in their own way. You can temper that fire!

Air Element: If you are Air element dominant, you may find that when you are out of balance you have a tendency to over intellectualise your experience, losing connection with your body and emotions in the process. In this case, bringing in some of water's sensuality may help calm your mind and allow you to settle into a more fully rounded present.

water element power spots

It might be obvious to suggest that people who have a strong Water element give themselves the opportunity to spend time near, in, or on the water on a regular basis. However, it is surprising how many Water people either do not recognise their need for this or do not take the initiative to make sure they do so.

To be at your best, if you are Water element dominant, spending time in or near your physical element – water – is vital to your wellbeing. In fact, I would state that it is you Water folk (along with those who identify strongly with Earth) who most need a regular immersion in their element. Balance for you means experiencing your element physically, not just thinking about it or imagining it. You must actually step into your watery sanctuary!

There are special places on earth where we can plug into our element and where particular elements are inordinately more powerful. The ancients were very aware of such places and often built temples or other religious structures on these special places of power.

For the Water element, these sacred places have extraordinary resonance:

- Magdalena Bay (USA/Mexico)
- Lake Wanaka (New Zealand)
- Lake Baikal (Russia)
- Fushimi Inari (Japan)
- The Tarkine (Australia)
- Amazonia (South America)
- The Ganges (India)

- Tanah Lot (Bali)
- Palenque (Mexico)
- Pu'uhonua (Hawaii)
- Sumba Island (Indonesia)

If you wish to read about these places, the energies they hold and how they might help you, you can learn more in my oracle deck *Earth Power: An Atlas for the Soul*.

the guidance

It is said that within 40 days and 40 nights profound change can be enacted and manifested. The following pieces of guidance flow from the deep-seated power of Water. They are designed to be considered, meditated on and absorbed one day at a time. Feel free to read through the entire section first, to get a feel for the messages as a whole. Then begin at the beginning, and give each one your focus, in turn, for a single day. Every day, let the messages work their magic upon and within you. Every day, you will change.

Receive.

40 days & 40 nights
of guidance
from the element
of water

1. I SHIMMER WITH THE RADIANCE OF BEING.

2 BREATHE DEEPLY AND THEN DIVE

3. WE ORIGINATED FROM WATER. I AM STILL FULL OF INNATE FLOW.

4. I TRUST THAT
I AM SUPPORTED,
ALWAYS,
AND SO I LET GO.

5. I AM ABUNDANT
AND CREATIVE.

6. I CHOOSE
TO RIPPLE
POSITIVITY
OUT INTO
THE
WORLD.

7. I CAN BE POWERFULLY GENTLE –
OR GENTLY POWERFUL.

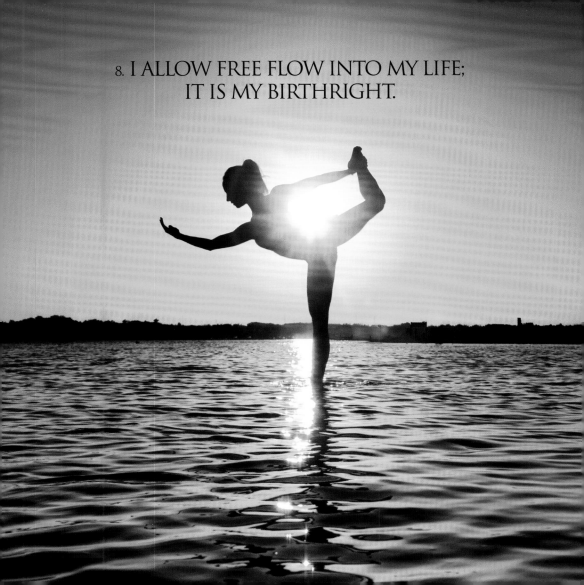

8. I ALLOW FREE FLOW INTO MY LIFE;
IT IS MY BIRTHRIGHT.

9. EVERYTHING CHANGES, AND I DO NOT RESIST THE CHANGE.

10. MY MIND IS CLEAR,
BRIGHT AND SHARP.

11. I FIND
FRIENDS
WHERE I LEAST
EXPECT TO.

12. THE INCOMING TIDE BRINGS ABUNDANCE.

THE OUTGOING TIDE TAKES WHAT I NO LONGER NEED.

13. I FLOW WITH THE RIVER,
NOT RESISTING THE PATH LIT FOR ME.

14. TO FLOAT ABOVE TURBULENT WATERS, WE MUST LET GO. WHEN WE ARE INFLEXIBLE AND TIGHT, WE SINK.

15.
I AM
FLUID
IN MY
THOUGHTS.

16. EVERY DAY
I AM SHOWERED IN GIFTS.

17. I HAVE A FOUNTAIN
OF WISDOM WITHIN ME.
I SIMPLY NEED TO ASK TO KNOW.

18.
EVEN THE MOST
RESISTANT ENERGY
IS SUBJECT
TO CHANGE.

19.
I AM
BUOYANT
AND
LIGHT-
HEARTED.

20. SEEK THOSE THINGS
THAT CLEAR YOUR MIND
AND WASH YOUR SPIRIT CLEAN.

21. I DO NOT DILUTE
MY HAPPINESS
WITH ANXIETY.

22. MY LOVE FOR MYSELF OVERFLOWS
AND RIPPLES OUTWARDS
TO ALL OTHERS.

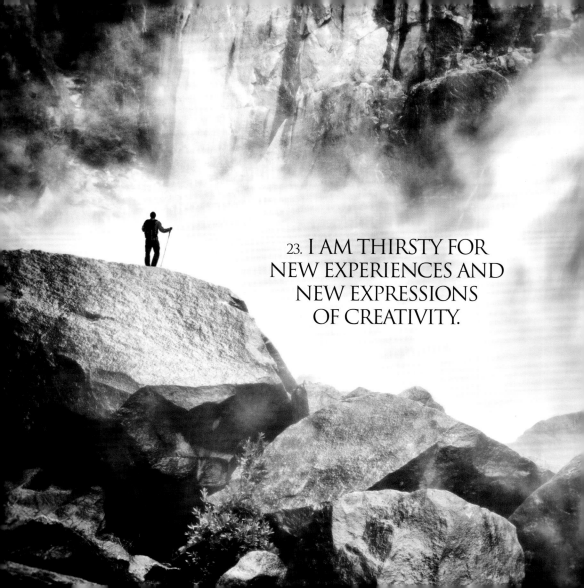

23. I AM THIRSTY FOR
NEW EXPERIENCES AND
NEW EXPRESSIONS
OF CREATIVITY.

24. I AM NOT AFRAID
TO DIVE DEEPLY.

25. I USE MY DISCERNMENT
TO CHOOSE WHEN TO SKIM PLAYFULLY
IN THE SHALLOWS.

26. I WASH AWAY WHAT IS NOT MINE.

27. A PEARL FORMS
AROUND AN IRRITATION.
IT BECOMES A PRECIOUS GIFT
OVER TIME.

29. I FLOW BRIGHTLY
TOWARDS MY PURPOSE.

30. I KNOW WHAT EMOTION I AM FEELING, WHEN I AM FEELING IT.

31. I CONTAIN
A RESERVOIR OF LOVE AND POWER.

32.
I MAKE
DECISIONS
WITH EASE
AND WISDOM.

33. I RELEASE MYSELF
TO EFFERVESCENCE
AND JOY.

34. I AM A REFLECTION OF THE DIVINE
IN ALL ITS DIVERSE FORMS.

35. I CAN SIT
PEACEFULLY
AND
EXPERIENCE A
QUIET DELUGE
OF LOVE FROM
ALL THINGS.

36. I TRUST THAT, WHILST I MAY NOT BE
ABLE TO SEE ALL THE WAY TO WHERE I
WANT TO GO, IT IS CERTAINLY THERE.

37. I AM UNIQUE AND
HAVE A STRONG PURPOSE.

38. I AM NOT AFRAID OF TRANSFORMATION.

39. I AM OPEN AND RESPONSIVE
TO THE VAST ABUNDANCE
OF THE UNIVERSE.

40. I DRENCH MYSELF
IN THE WONDERS OF LIFE.

summary of traditional correspondences for the elements

AIR
- Direction: North
- Incense, fragrance, smoke, kites, balloons, oils such as bergamot, lime, eucalyptus
- Smudging, blowing smoke, bubbles, ringing bells, singing bowls
- Communication, creativity, logic, travel, new beginnings, ideas, flow
- Colours: white, yellow, silver
- Time: dawn

WATER
- Direction: South
- Salt water, moon water, shells, rain, oils such as water lily, ylang ylang
- Anointing with water, passing the cup, diving deep
- Relationships, love, psychic connection, birth/death/rebirth
- Feminine, associated with the moon
- Colours: blue and grey
- Time: dusk

FIRE
- Direction: East
- Candles, open flame of any kind, oils such as pepper, ginger, frankincense
- Lighting flame, passing flame around the circle, anointing with warming oil
- Passion, purpose, strength, achievement, destruction of what is not needed
- Masculine, associated with the sun
- Colours: red and orange
- Time: noon

EARTH
- Direction: West
- Salt, earth, clay, oils such as oak moss, patchouli, frankincense
- Standing on the earth, walking barefoot, wearing flower crowns, sprinkling of earth and salt
- Resilience, order, law, politics, education, security, money
- Colours: green and brown
- Time: night

australian alternatives to elemental directions and associations

Air: West – mountains
Water: East – ocean on coast
Fire: North – equator
Earth: South – ice mass

about the author

STACEY DEMARCO is an internationally respected pagan spiritual practitioner and author who hails from Sydney, Australia. Her passion is making practical magic accessible to everyone and reconnecting people with the power of nature. She has a down-to-earth yet scholarly approach to magic and is skilled at weaving together ancient techniques to solve modern problems. Stacey has a dedicated clientele and enjoys popularity as a regular contributor on all things spiritual across television, radio and other media.

Once described by the Australian mainstream financial press as the "thinking woman's witch," Stacey is the author of three best selling books on earth-based spirituality, including the classic *Witch in the Boardroom*. Her annual *Lunar & Seasonal Diary for the Southern Hemisphere* is eagerly awaited each year.

A long time lover and scholar of the mythos of the feminine and masculine divine, her first set of oracle cards, *Gods & Titans*, illustrated by awardwinning artist Jimmy Manton, was released in early 2011, and her second set, *Goddesses & Sirens*, was released later the same year. Her love of nature and travel is reflected in her deck *Earth Power: An Atlas for the Soul*, released in 2014, followed by her stunning *Halloween Oracle*, based on the power available on the most magical night of the year. Stacey's *The Gospel of Aradia*, an oracle deck based on Aradia, the first of all witches, also came out in 2016. In 2017, Stacey's *Viking Oracle* was released.

Stacey teaches, consults and holds workshops and retreats in Australia and around the world. She lives on a cliff by the sea with her husband and animal companions. Active in the pagan community, she is the founder of Natureluster, a science-based programme that assists people to heal themselves through the power of nature. She is an avid adventure traveller and beekeeper, loves messing around with photography and on mountains and is a very average skier. About the latter, she has now fully accepted there will be no great improvement. Ever.

Join her on **www.facebook/staceydemarco**
or at **www.themodernwitch.com**

notes

notes

notes

notes

notes

For more information on this
or any Blue Angel Publishing release,
please visit our website at:

www.blueangelonline.com